THE
TIMEWARP
TRIALS

GUY FAWKES
GUILTY OR INNOCENT?

Stewart Ross
illustrated by Élisabeth Eudes-Pascal

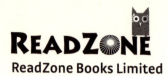

READZONE

ReadZone Books Limited

First published in this edition 2017

© copyright in the text Stewart Ross 2011
© copyright in this edition ReadZone Books 2017

First published 2011 by Evans Brothers Ltd

The right of the Author to be identified as the Author of this work
has been asserted by the Author in accordance with the Copyright,
Designs and Patents Act 1988.

Printed in Malta by Melita Press

British Library Cataloguing in Publication Data (CIP) is available
for this title.

ISBN 978-1-78322-633-7

Visit our website: www.readzonebooks.com

THE TIMEWARP TRIALS

GUY FAWKES
GUILTY OR INNOCENT?

Stewart Ross
illustrated by Élisabeth Eudes-Pascal

Defendant

DOCK

Judge,
The Honourable
Ms Winifred Wigmore

Prosecuting lawyer,
Miss Tankia Bessant

CLERK
Mr George S. Cribble

PUBLIC GALLERY/PRESS

The High Court of History

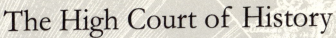

Witness

WITNESS BOX

Defence lawyer,
Mr Leroy Williams

JURY

In the beginning…

DOCTOR DAVID GIBBON glanced down at his phone to see who was calling. "Horatio G" was flashing on the screen. He pressed the answer button. 'Horatio, how are you?'

Professor Geekmeister had never been one for small talk. 'David,' he said earnestly, 'who's next?'

Doc David's mind whirled. What on earth was the professor on about? He might have the biggest brain on the planet but, like a wonky supermarket trolley, it wasn't always easy to follow where it was going.

'Sorry Horatio. Who is to be what next?'

'Oh really, David! Come along! Who shall I bring back next to appear before the High Court of History?'

Ah! thought Doc David, the country's leading historian, so Horatio's up to his old tricks again, is he? Not surprising. The trial of King Henry VIII had been such a success. All around the world millions had followed every moment on TVs, laptops and phones, and the DVD had sold over a billion. No wonder old Geekmeister wanted to have another go....

David's thoughts were interrupted by the professor. 'Well, David? I rely on you, you know. So come along. Who shall I try to bring back to life this time? Someone like George Washington?'

'No!' howled Doc David. 'You can't put Washington on trial!'

'Why not? He was a rebel and a slave owner. Sounds a pretty nasty piece of work to me.'

Doc David took a deep breath. 'Listen, Horatio. Take my word for it, George Washington would not be suitable. For a start, the Americans would go crazy. They've named their capital city after him, haven't they? It'd be like putting the entire USA on trial.'

'Well....'

'No, just don't go there, Horatio. Choose a safer option, someone like Guy Fawkes.'

There was a long pause. Eventually, Doc David asked, 'Don't like the idea? Much safer bet than George Washington.'

'I know. I love the idea of Guy Fawkes.'

'So?'

'I'm just not sure where I could find a sample of his DNA.'

'Mmm,' mused Doc David. 'Tricky. As far as I know, no bits of his body were ever preserved. Nor his belongings – at least, not in this country. Wait a minute....'

'Yes? Go on!'

'Around 1602 or 03 he went to Spain. I remember hearing somewhere that a church near Toledo claims to have an item of his clothing… a hat, I think. It's preserved as a holy relic. Fawkes was a Roman Catholic, you see, and in their eyes....'

Professor Geekmeister had stopped listening. A hat! On it, maybe a flake of dandruff? Enough to get a sample of DNA. Just a single molecule would do. He must get hold of Guy Fawkes' hat!

And he did. After months of searching, the professor's faithful researchers came up with what he wanted. How they did it, no one knows. There is a story that the parish priest of Santa Maria, Bargas, near Toledo, suddenly inherited a small fortune from an unknown aunt and went to live in South America. His congregation also say that, around the same time, a battered old hat, kept for centuries in

a glass case in the church's crypt, had been miraculously transformed into a new one. There is no evidence to back up either story.

Nevertheless, somehow and from somewhere, Horatio Geekmeister found a trace of Guy Fawkes' DNA. From it, using his secret process, he brought the man back to stand trial in the High Court of History.

The Accused

'WE ARE ASSEMBLED HERE,' announced Judge Wigmore in her no-nonsense tones, 'to try the case of Mr Guy Fawkes, sometimes known as Mr Guido Fawkes.'

A slight muttering from the public gallery was silenced by a single dart from Ms Wigmore's icy blue eyes. 'Clerk?'

George S. Cribble stood up as quickly as his spindly legs would allow. 'Here, My Lady.'

'Very good. Right, Mr Cribble, you may bring in the accused.'

'Certainly, My Lady.' Signalling to the two burly security men to come with him, Cribble left the court.

While the clerk was gone, The Honourable Ms Winifred Wigmore surveyed the scene before her. As for the last trial in the High Court of History, the public gallery and the press box were both crammed to bursting. Above her, the fish-eye lenses of the TV cameras scanned the courtroom. They were looking for someone interesting, a celebrity perhaps, to zoom in on.

The jury was seated to the judge's left. Some of the dozen members were nervously tidying their hair, while others were jotting things down on the notepads they had been given. A round-faced man with flat, greasy hair was trying to get the attention of the young woman beside him. From the look on her face, it was clear she was not interested.

The four children on the jury – chosen because Professor Geekmeister believed that children were better judges of character than adults – were whispering eagerly among themselves.

'Weird, eh?' a curly-headed girl named Jasmine was saying to the boy with glasses sitting next to her. 'Like being in a movie.'

'Better,' the boy replied.

Jasmine nodded.

Before long, the sound of the clerk's footsteps could be heard coming back down the corridor. Cribble entered seconds later and sat down. Standing by the door, Sergeant Vanwall glanced over his shoulder before barking with his usual ferocity, 'Silence! Silence in court!' All eyes were riveted on the opening beside him.

As Guy Fawkes strode into the court, a gasp of surprise ran around the public gallery. Especially from the ladies. Instead of the small, mean-looking man most people had been expecting, the accused was tall and powerful, almost noble in appearance. Thick reddish-brown hair, the colour of autumn leaves, flowed from beneath a broad-rimmed felt hat. Above a beard the same warm hue as his hair, his mouth seemed to quiver slightly, as if about to break into a smile.

All in all, he was a most handsome, dashing-looking fellow.

Judge Wigmore, however, was not impressed.

'Mr Fawkes, do you have no respect for my court?' she demanded as the security men showed him to his place in the dock.

Guy Fawkes looked surprised. 'I have as much respect for your court, My Lady, as for any other court on earth.'

For a fraction of a second, the judge seemed lost for words. 'I'm glad to hear it,' she replied. 'Then kindly remove your hat!'

'I apologise if it gives offence, My Lady,' said Fawkes, removing it with a flourish that sent his long hair bouncing over his muscular shoulders. 'I come from a different century and have not quite mastered the customs of this one.'

'I understand, Mr Fawkes. Now to the matter in hand. You are accused of being a terrorist. Please inform the court how you wish to plead.'

'A terrorist?' Fawkes questioned. 'What is that, My Lady?'

Once again the defendant's words appeared to surprise the judge. 'A terrorist,' she explained, 'is someone who uses terror as a way of getting what they want. So, how do you plead?'

Fawkes smiled. 'Using – terror – to – get – what – I – wanted?' he repeated slowly. 'Well, at my last trial, when I was accused of treason, I pleaded "not guilty". I shall do the same now, and hope that this time justice will be done.'

'It certainly will,' retorted Judge Wigmore. 'No one has ever questioned the justice of my court.'

'Thank you, My Lady,' Fawkes replied. 'That will be a change!'

Over in the jury box, Jasmine wrote *Cool guy?* on her pad in large scrawly letters.

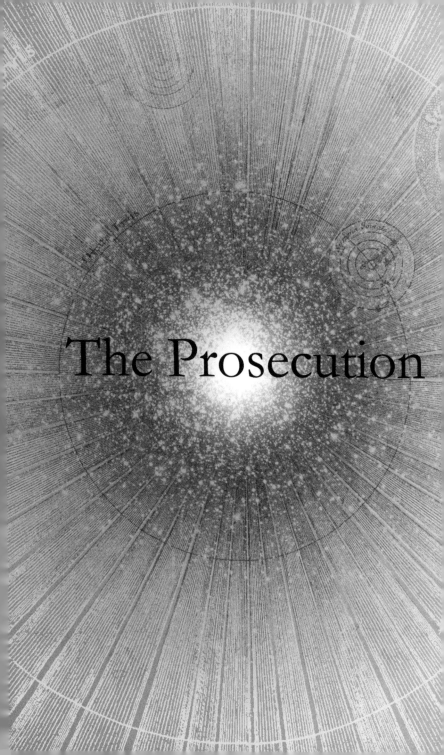

The Prosecution

AS IN ALL TRIALS in the High Court of History, the prosecution was carried out by Tankia Bessant. A raven-haired, hook-nosed lady of about forty, it was her aim to prove Guy Fawkes guilty of being a terrorist. The final decision, though, would be made by the twelve men, women and children of the jury.

When she had first heard whom she would be prosecuting and what for, Miss Bessant had let out a little cry of delight. Guy Fawkes a terrorist? Everyone who had ever heard of him knew he was guilty. She had never had such an easy case.

'Mr Fawkes,' she began, walking towards him in shoes that clicked on the court's hard floor, 'let me explain in detail the case against you.'

'Please do,' he replied with the same politeness as he had shown towards the judge. 'That would be most kind.'

'Good. You were born in York on 13th April 1570 and were educated at St Peter's School in that city?'

'That is true, Miss Bessant.'

'And did the masters at this school teach you that murder is a crime and a sin?'

'Indeed they did, Miss Bessant.'

'And did they also teach you that you owe all worldly obedience to His Majesty The King?'

Yet again a smile played across Guy Fawkes' lips. 'Not exactly, no. At that time England was ruled by a queen, Miss Bessant, not a king. Queen Elizabeth I. But they did try to teach me to honour and obey her.'

Tankia Bessant looked annoyed. She did not like being caught out. 'Try to teach you? Would you explain please, Mr Fawkes?'

'Well, my schoolmaster said that our queen was the most important person in the land and I should say prayers for her and so on. I believed him, but later I saw how wrong he was.'

Ah! This was the reply Prosecutor Bessant had been waiting for. Very carefully, step by step, she pieced together Guy Fawkes' first life. How he had changed his religion to become a Roman Catholic and then served as a Catholic soldier, fighting for the Spanish army in Europe.

'You were rather a good soldier, weren't you, Mr Fawkes?' she asked. 'A bit of an expert?'

'Some said so, yes,' he replied modestly.

'And what did you specialise in?'

'Explosives, Miss Bessant. Blowing things up.'

Tankia Bessant turned to the jury. 'Please remember that, ladies, gentlemen and children. Mr Fawkes was an expert in blowing things up.'

Tom, the boy with the glasses, nodded and wrote on his pad, *GF Xpert with gunpowder B4 joined plot*. His teacher, Miss Fine, wouldn't like it but shortened 'text speak' did have its uses.

The prosecutor then outlined how the accused had been recruited by Thomas Winter to help with a plot to blow up Parliament when the king, the nobility and most of the government were inside. Fawkes denied none of this.

By this stage Tankia Bessant was getting a bit confused by Fawkes' answers.

'Let me get this clear, Mr Fawkes,' she said. 'You admit that you were a key part of a plot to blow up the House of Lords when the king was there?'

Fawkes nodded.

'That you were found under the House of Lords coming out of a cellar in which thirty-six barrels of gunpowder had been hidden?'

Again Fawkes nodded.

'And you still say that you are not a terrorist?'

Fawkes nodded for a third time.

'Then how on earth,' Miss Bessant concluded, 'can you say you are not guilty?'

At this point Judge Wigmore decided it was time she joined in. No one, she said, was keener than herself to see justice done. But did the accused, Mr Fawkes, understand what he was saying? Did he realise what he was admitting? He was as good as saying he was guilty of terrorism.

Guy Fawkes raised his right hand as if asking permission to speak in class. 'May I say something, My Lady?'

'Say as much as you like, Mr Fawkes,' said the judge. 'It had better be good or Mr Williams is going to find it very difficult to defend you.'

'Yes,' chipped in Miss Bessant. 'Fire away – although that might not be the best thing to say to a soldier.'

Fawkes smiled. 'Thank you, My Lady. And thank you, Miss Bessant. You are both much more understanding than the last people to prosecute me.' He looked around the court. 'They used torture, ladies and gentlemen, to try to get me to betray my friends. I was tortured on the rack. I will not go into the details, but it brought pain beyond your imagining.'

By now all four children on the jury were looking most uncomfortable. Jasmine had turned green and, thinking she was going to be sick, asked to leave the room. The judge ordered a five-minute break for her to recover.

'You OK?' asked Tom when she came back into the jury box.

'Yes thanks. Just not very good with the gruesome bits.'

'Me neither. Do you think he said it to get sympathy?'

Jasmine thought for a moment. 'Mmm, maybe. I just can't make him out.'

With everyone back in their places and Jasmine now a healthier colour, Fawkes continued. 'I am accused of being a terrorist. That is, of using terror to get what I wanted. The first part of the charge I agree with. I did use, or rather I planned to use, terror. I admit that I was part of a plot to blow up Parliament.'

'I think we have reached that point already,' interrupted Tankia Bessant. 'But go on, Mr Fawkes. Go on.'

'Very well, Miss Bessant. Listen very carefully, please.' Fawkes glanced in the direction of the jury, then turned to face the judge. 'My Lady, this court must believe me when I say that I did not plot to blow up Parliament to get what I wanted.'

'Ah!' interrupted the prosecutor again. 'So you are saying you were tricked into it?'

'Tricked, Miss Bessant? Not at all. I knew exactly what I was doing.' Fawkes paused and lifted his eyes towards the ceiling. 'I was doing what God wanted. I was doing God's will.'

A stunned silence fell across the entire court. No one moved. No one said a word because no one knew what to say.

Tankia Bessant was the first to find her voice. 'Let me get this straight, Mr Fawkes. You admit to being a terrorist – but a terrorist for God. You knew what God wanted better than any of those you were going to blow up?'

Fawkes looked her straight in the eye. 'Miss Bessant, I knew exactly what God wanted. He wanted me to blow up the wicked Protestant king and replace him with a true Catholic one.'

'Right,' Tankia Bessant snapped. 'I know just what to do about that.' She turned to the judge. 'My Lady, I would like to call my witness, His Majesty King James the First!'

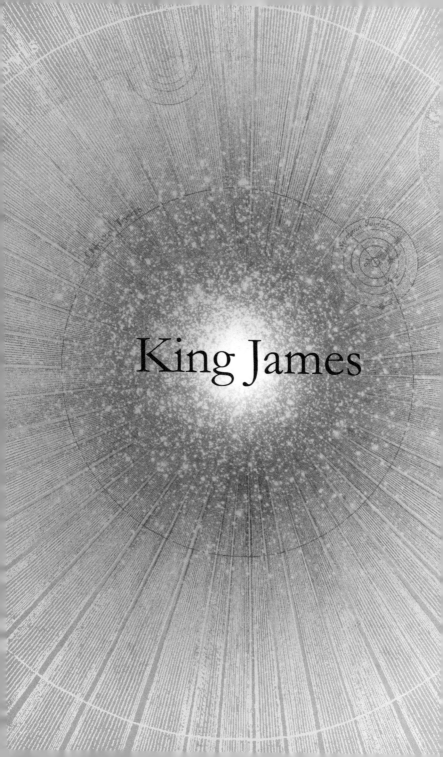

King James

'MAJESTY' WAS NOT A WORD that came immediately to mind on first seeing James Stuart. Although a double king – King James the Sixth of Scotland and James the First of England – he did not look very royal. He was neither tall nor powerful. His hair was straggly, his beard thin, his eyes somewhat bulgy and his manners appalling. But what he lacked in appearance, he made up for in brains. King James was very, very learned – although this was not always obvious when he spoke.

James' entrance into the court was so ridiculous that it made the children in the jury giggle. He minced into the room, stopped, stared about him, took off his hat, which had a long blue peacock feather stuck in the top, waved it to the gallery, and then bowed to the judge so clumsily that he almost fell over. He needed, or pretended he needed, one of the security men to take his arm and help him into the witness box. There he sat, reeking of perfume, his hands resting delicately on an elegantly crossed knee.

'Your Majesty,' began Tankia Bessant, approaching the witness box, 'we are so pleased that you are here to help us today.'

The king raised an eyebrow. 'Don't be silly! I had no choice, woman.'

The Honourable Ms Winifred Wigmore slapped her hand firmly on the desk before her. 'Mr Stuart, you will remember where you are, please!'

'I am not a fool, lady!' James retorted. 'I know very well where I am: in the High Court of History in the twenty-first century. Correct?'

'Correct, Mr Stuart. And in a court of law you show respect to the officials by calling them by their right names. You will refer to

me as "My Lady" and to the prosecuting lawyer as Miss Bessant or simply "madam". Do you understand?'

'De minimis non curat rex,' muttered James. 'But I will obey. My Lady.'

'Good. And another thing, Mr Stuart….'

'Yes?'

'Kindly do not show off by speaking Latin in my court, especially when you are using it to be rude.'

James held up his hands in mock amazement. 'You understood, My Lady?'

'I did. You said, "A king does not concern himself with trivial things." The High Court of History is not trivial, Mr Stuart. And you are no longer a king. You were one, but now you are an ex-king and you will obey my law. Or, if you'd prefer it in Latin, dura lex, sed lex – "The law may be harsh, but it is still the law". Don't forget.'

To everyone's amazement, James took out a pink silk handkerchief and began dabbing tears from his eyes.

'I'm so sorry, My Lady,' he sniffed. 'Don't be cross with me, please. I'm only a poor wee boy who lost his mother when he was a baby. All alone in the world.…'

Tom and Jasmine both stared in amazement at James' behaviour. Tankia Bessant was less tolerant. 'Your Majesty!' she said firmly. 'Please get a grip on yourself!'

James peered at her sorrowfully over the top of his handkerchief. 'Aye, Miss Bessant. Dear Miss Bessant, I will.'

'Good. Now I would be very grateful if you would answer a few questions. First, do you recognise that man over there?'

She pointed to where Guy Fawkes stood at the other side of the court.

James tucked his handkerchief neatly into his sleeve and, taking his time, turned towards the dock. Immediately his eyes fell on Fawkes, he let out a piercing scream. 'No! It's him!' he shouted, cowering up against the side of the witness box like a terrified chick before a hungry fox.

'Who?' demanded Tankia Bessant.

'Fawkes! The frightful Fawkes! The demon who tried to kill me with gunpowder!'

'Ah. But Fawkes says, Your Majesty, that he was only trying to do what God wanted.'

'What God wanted?!' cried James, so carried away that he almost fell off his chair. 'God wanted me! Kings are – were – appointed by God to look after His people. I was the loving father of the British people, as God demanded. As I once rather wisely said, deo rex, a rege lex… Oops! I mean: "The king is from God, and the law is from the king."'

Tankia Bessant folded her arms and walked over to stand before the jury. 'Honest members of the community,' she said carefully, 'we seem to have a problem. Mr Fawkes says God wanted him to kill the king, while His Majesty says God wanted him to be king. Who are we to believe?'

'Me! Me! Me, good lady!' burst out James. 'My people agreed, too. When they heard that I had been saved from the dastardly gunpowder plot, they rang the church bells and danced in the street, and ever since then they have celebrated the day I was saved – November the fifth – with bonfires and fireworks. Would God allow such a thing if He had wanted me blown to pieces? Could the whole nation possibly be wrong and just that fellow Fawkes be right?'

Tankia Bessant turned to Guy Fawkes. 'Well, Mr Fawkes, what do you say to that?'

'The whole nation did not rejoice,' he replied, looking very dignified. 'Some Roman Catholics thought it a tragedy that we failed.'

'Only a few?'

'Yes, only a few. But the few may be right and the many wrong.'

The prosecutor showed what she thought of this idea by ignoring it completely. After a few more questions, she allowed King James to leave the court and began her summing up to the jury.

The case was simple, she explained. Guy Fawkes had admitted that he had tried to blow up Parliament, with the king and hundreds of other people inside it. That was a terrible thing to want to do. It was terrorism, plain and simple. And it was no excuse to say he believed God wanted him to do it.

'If I stole a car,' Tankia Bessant asked, 'and then told the police, when they arrested me, that God had wanted me to steal it, would that mean I had been right? No, of course it would not! No one can say for certain what God wants. Indeed, some people don't even believe in God.

'So, honest members of the community, there is only one verdict you can reach. That man over there, Guy Fawkes, is wicked. He is conceited, too, because he says he was right and almost everyone else in the country was wrong.

'Fawkes is guilty, ladies and gentlemen. As clearly—'

Miss Bessant's words were interrupted by a cough from the judge, who pointed towards the jury.

'Ah yes!' the lawyer muttered, looking a bit irritated. 'I apologise. I will start again.

'Fawkes is guilty, ladies, gentlemen and children of the jury. As clearly as he stands before you, he is guilty of being an evil, cruel, heartless terrorist!'

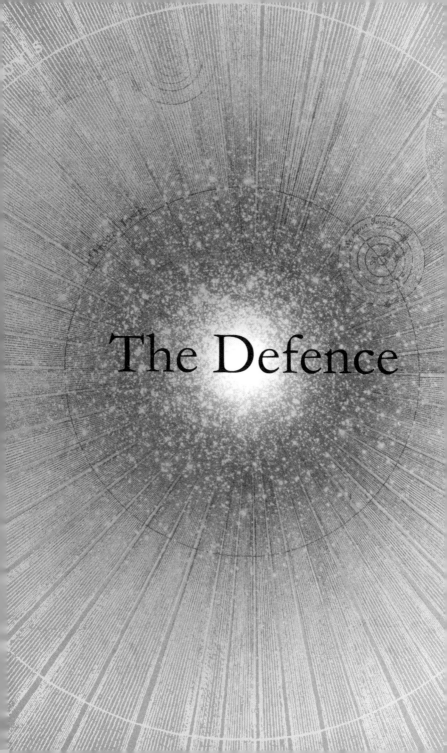

The Defence

DEFENCE LAWYER Leroy Williams had handled some tricky cases in his time, but never one quite as tricky as this. Guy Fawkes had said that he was not guilty, yet he had confessed to trying to blow up Parliament. Strange, annoying even. But not an impossible position, the defence lawyer thought to himself as he prepared his case. It all depended on how it was presented....

After Tankia Bessant sat down, Leroy Williams waited a while before getting to his feet. When he eventually did so, his face was lit by a broad smile. He bowed to the judge and walked over to the jury.

'Ladies, gentlemen and children – my friends, if I may call you that – I know what you are thinking. You reckon there is no point in my even trying to defend Guy Fawkes because he has admitted being part of the Gunpowder Plot. True. But has he admitted to being a terrorist? No, he has not! I ask you, therefore, to listen to me with open minds.

'Mr Fawkes,' the lawyer continued, strolling over to the dock, 'you admit plotting to destroy most of the Parliament building?'

'I do, Mr Williams.'

The lawyer became more serious. 'And you admit that the explosion would have killed and injured dozens, perhaps even hundreds of people?'

'I do, Mr Williams.'

'Many of those you planned to kill were innocent. Some were even Roman Catholics, like yourself. How did that make you feel? Happy or sad?'

For the first time, Guy Fawkes allowed his head to drop. His voice fell to almost a whisper as he replied, 'Sad, Mr Williams. Very, very sad.'

'Go on, Mr Fawkes. Why?'

'I do not expect you or anyone else in this court to understand. But I love my country and I wanted to help it.'

By now Leroy Williams was standing right next to the dock, leaning against it and talking almost directly into Guy Fawkes' ear. 'You wanted to help the English people by killing their king?'

'Yes. With King James out of the way, we planned to set up a Roman Catholic monarch,

James' younger son Charles or his daughter Elizabeth. Then the people would have been free again and their souls would have been saved from hell.'

Williams stepped back and scratched his head. 'Saved from hell, yes. But what about the explosion, the murder, the pain, the misery-'

'Yes, yes,' Fawkes interrupted. 'I know. But it would have been like cutting off a poisoned leg, a little pain to save the whole body.'

Running his hand over his hair, Williams repeated, 'You wanted to cut off a leg to save the body, Mr Fawkes? You were not a killer but a saviour?'

The defendant replied with a long speech about his life as a soldier. In the wars he had seen many buildings, even whole towns blown up and many people, innocent as well as guilty, horribly killed. But that is what happened when good and evil were in conflict. Doing some study since Professor Geekmeister had brought him back to life, he had learned about what had happened in the world since his death.

'I read that in your last great war,' he explained, 'two cities were entirely destroyed by gigantic bombs. Thousands of innocent people died. Those who caused the explosions said they were horrible but necessary – they allowed good to triumph over evil. I felt just the same all those many years ago, in the autumn of 1605.'

Leroy Williams nodded. 'So you say you are not a terrorist but a warrior for good against evil?'

'That is so, Mr Williams.'

The lawyer turned to the judge. 'My Lady, I would at this point like to call my witness, Mr Robert Catesby.'

All through the examination Tom had been writing furiously in his pad. First he had written, *GF admits!!!*

Then came a few more jottings and some interesting doodles before *Like terrorists 2day??* Then *They say doin rite – we say doin rong! Who nose wots rite?* followed by still more notes and jottings.

Finally, at the end, he wrote, *I just don't no!!!* and underlined it five times.

A few minutes later a tall, good-looking young man walked briskly into the room, bowed his head slightly towards the judge and took his place in the witness box. What followed surprised everybody in the court, Guy Fawkes more than most.

Robert Catesby

LEROY WILLIAMS STARTED by checking that the man in the witness box really was the leader of the Gunpowder Plot.

Yes, Catesby confirmed, he and his cousin, Thomas Winter, had dreamed up the idea. They hoped that once Parliament had been blown up and the king killed, the whole country would rise up behind them. They had stored the gunpowder in Catesby's house before rowing it across the Thames at night and hiding it beneath the Parliament building. Catesby, too, had decided that Guy Fawkes was just the man to help them.

'Ah!' exclaimed the lawyer. 'Why did you choose Mr Fawkes?'

'Precisely the kind of chap we needed,' replied Catesby in a rather jaunty manner. As he was speaking, he smiled across at his ex-colleague in the dock. 'First, he was a terrific soldier, a real expert in gunpowder and how to set it off and all that sort of thing.'

'Go on, please.'

'Second, he was such a brick.'

'A brick?' interrupted the judge, suddenly coming to life. 'Are you saying Mr Fawkes was a piece of masonry?'

'No. Sorry, My Lady. Professor Geekmeister must have got some of my vocabulary muddled when he was programming me. What I mean is that Fawkes was a frightfully good chap. One of the best. Patient, cheerful, loyal and tremendously religious. I never heard him swear, and he was always saying little prayers. One of the best, I'd say.'

'Thank you, Mr Catesby,' said Leroy Williams. 'My friends of the jury, you have heard someone who knew the accused very well describe him as a good, honest man. "One of the best," were the words he used. I would like you to remember that, please.'

He turned back to his witness. 'Now Mr Catesby, if it is not too painful for you, I would like you to tell us about the last hour or so of your life. Your first life, of course.'

'Gosh! Well, I'll do my best. I was shot dead, you see.'

'I know.'

'It didn't really hurt, surprisingly. I suppose I was too shocked. Anyway, by then I knew it was all over. Actually, I had lost my nerve a bit after that business with the gunpowder.'

The lawyer looked at him sharply. 'You mean the gunpowder hidden under Parliament? I thought that had been discovered.'

'It had, yes. I mean the gunpowder we wanted to use for our guns.'

'What happened to it?'

Looking a bit sheepish, Catesby explained how he and his fellow plotters had decided to make a last stand in Holbeach House in Staffordshire. As their supply of gunpowder had got a bit damp, they tried drying it out in front of the fire.

'Yes, yes, I know!' he said. 'A pretty daft thing to do, eh? But we were all in such a state by then that we hardly knew what we were doing. The plot had failed, we had been chased across the countryside and were now surrounded.'

'So what happened to the gunpowder?' asked Leroy Williams.

'Well, you can guess, can't you? A small spark from the fire and... boom! The whole lot went up, blowing a hole in the roof. One chap was blinded and most of the rest of us were injured in some way. I was badly burned on the arm.'

At this point Catesby's mood changed. 'It was not the burn that upset me, Mr Williams, so much as what had happened. It was as if someone had been trying to tell us something.'

Once more the court room fell completely silent. Tom nudged Jasmine. The judge, the galleries, even Tankia Bessant and Guy Fawkes leaned forward to catch every word Catesby uttered.

'Someone had been trying to tell you something, Mr Catesby?' asked his lawyer quietly. 'Would you explain, please?'

'Don't you see? We had planned to blow up the king with gunpowder – and instead we had blown ourselves up! Ironic or what, eh? We thought God had been guiding our hands in the plot. So when it was us and

not the king who suffered, we realised that God was telling us that our explosion idea was not very sensible. We'd been wrong from the start!'

A low moan came from the dock, where Guy Fawkes sat with his head in his hands.

'Sorry Guy, old fellow. But I reckon it was all a mistake. Should never have asked you to join us. My fault. Terribly sorry, really am.'

What a business! thought Jasmine. You could never make it up – no one would believe you. It's difficult not to feel a bit sorry for the poor old guy, just a bit… But what would have happened if they hadn't caught him? Like a seventeenth-century Twin Towers….

When Robert Catesby had left the court, Leroy Williams summed up his position.

'Ladies, gentlemen and children of the jury,' he began, 'or should I call you guys and girls?'

'No you should not!' cut in Judge Wigmore. 'You will kindly address the jury in the correct manner, Mr Williams.'

'I apologise, My Lady. I was trying to make a point about "guys". Nowadays the word "guy" is used all over the world to mean a person, any person but usually a male one. It is a friendly, pleasant term. And it comes from the man standing in the dock, Guy Fawkes.'

When she heard this, Jasmine leaned across to Tom and whispered, 'I never knew that!'

'Neither did I,' he replied. 'I wonder if it's true?'

Their conversation was stopped by a fierce look from the judge.

'And the word "guy" is used everywhere,' Leroy Williams went on, 'to mean an agreeable fellow. And Mr Fawkes is an agreeable fellow, as we have seen for ourselves and as Mr Catesby has told us. Is that a terrorist?'

The lawyer then said that Fawkes had not actually done anything wrong, either. He had plotted, he had planned but he had been arrested before doing any harm. Was that a terrorist?

Guy Fawkes had not sought glory or wealth. He had simply done what he believed God wanted. He acted out of consideration towards his fellow human beings, not out of spite or cruelty.

'Finally,' the defence lawyer concluded, 'I would suggest that Mr Fawkes, a good man, was led astray – no, please don't interrupt me, Mr Fawkes – by Mr Catesby and others. He was a humble soldier, they were gentlemen. One of them, Thomas Percy, was a cousin of the Earl of Northumberland. I suggest that Fawkes, a man of honour, was flattered when a band of smart and wealthy young men asked him for help. He accepted their invitation when he should, of course, have turned it down.

'Just before his death, Catesby realised what a fool he had been. Fawkes was too true, too honourable for that. He was a man of principle. He suffered terribly at the hands of his torturers and died for his one mistake.

'Is that the portrait of a terrorist, my dear friends? I suggest not. Guy Fawkes is no villain but a good man who got into the wrong company. In short, he is innocent of the charge made against him.'

So that she could collect her thoughts, The Honourable Ms Winifred Wigmore gave the court a half-hour break. When it was over and everyone was back in their places, she handed down her instructions to the jury. This was, she reminded them, a very difficult case.

They had heard what a terrorist was. The prosecuting lawyer, Miss Tankia Bessant, had argued strongly that Guy Fawkes obviously was a terrorist. He had as good as admitted it himself, she said. Mr Leroy Williams, on the other hand, had pointed out that Fawkes had never admitted to being a terrorist. Instead, the defence had said he was more to be pitied than punished.

'So there you have it,' said the judge, taking off her reading glasses and putting them away in a small tartan case. 'Members of the jury, you must now reach a decision. If you find Mr Fawkes guilty, he will spend the rest of his second life behind bars. If you find him not guilty, he will be free to follow a normal life.

'I now ask you to retire from the court to reach your verdict.'

Dear Reader,

YOU are a member of the jury!

You were one of the two children sitting behind Jasmine and Tom.

If you go to my website **www.stewartross.com**, you can get in touch and tell me your decision: Guy Fawkes, guilty or not guilty of being a terrorist?

I will write back and let you know how others have voted. And when we have enough votes, I'll put a page on my website announcing the verdict: Guy Fawkes, guilty or innocent?

I do hope you enjoyed this book. If you did, you might like the others in the Timewarp Trials series.

Best wishes

The Gunpowder Plot

1547-1553 Reign of King Edward VI: England changes to the Protestant religion.

1553-1558 Reign of Queen Mary I: England changes back to the Roman Catholic religion.

1558-1603 Reign of Queen Elizabeth I: England Protestant once again.

1570 Guy Fawkes born in York.

1592 Fawkes goes to the Netherlands to fight in the Roman Catholic army of Spain.

1603 Queen Elizabeth I dies. King James VI of Scotland becomes King James I of England. James, a Protestant, is less tolerant towards Roman Catholics than they had expected. Fawkes visits Spain to ask for help for England's Roman Catholics.

1604 Robert Catesby and Thomas Winter ask Fawkes to help with their plot to kill the King by blowing up Parliament.

Plotters begin to dig a tunnel underneath the House of Lords. Number of plotters increases.

1605   Plotters hire a cellar beneath the House of Lords and abandon their tunnel. Fawkes, calling himself 'John Johnson', hides almost one ton of gunpowder beneath firewood in the cellar. One of the plotters, probably Francis Tresham, sends an anonymous letter to Lord Monteagle, a Roman Catholic. It warns him to stay away from the opening of Parliament. Monteagle alerts the King. **5 November**, date set for the opening of Parliament. Search party finds Fawkes and the gunpowder. Fawkes arrested and tortured to reveal details of the plot. Remaining plotters killed or arrested.

1606   **January**. Eight plotters tried for high treason. All found guilty and executed.

Guy Fawkes and history

Roman Catholics and Protestants

For about 1,500 years, the Christians of Western Europe belonged to the Roman Catholic Church. It was headed by the Pope, who lived in Rome, and its followers believed in more or less the same things. In the early years of the 16th century (1501-1600), the Roman Catholic Church split. Large numbers of Christians no longer shared the Pope's beliefs, and they did not accept him as their leader. The break-away Christians were known as 'Protestants'; those remaining in the Roman Catholic Church were called simply 'Catholics'.

Protestants and Catholics each believed their version of Christianity was the true one. They hated each other and fought long, bitter and bloody wars.

Protestant England

During the middle years of the 16th century, England swung back and forth between Protestant and Catholic. Finally, when Elizabeth I became Queen in 1558, the country attached itself firmly to the Protestant camp. Foreign Catholics attacked

England and tried to replace Elizabeth with her Catholic cousin, Mary.

Elizabeth survived. After her death, the throne of England passed to James I, the Protestant King of Scotland. By now, England's Catholics were getting desperate because they feared England would never again be a Catholic country. At this point, Robert Catesby and Thomas Winter hit upon the idea of a plot to blow up Parliament when the Protestant King was inside the building. As they were not explosives experts, they asked Guy Fawkes, a Catholic soldier, to help them…

History, the search for truth

Neither of the two lawyers in this book – Tanka Bessant and Leroy Williams – tell lies. They both argue using historical facts: there was a Catholic plot to blow up Parliament with James I inside it, Guy Fawkes was part of this plot, and he did hide barrels of gunpowder in a cellar under the Parliament building.

But history is not just knowing facts; it's about deciding how important they are and what they mean. For example, nowadays Protestants and Catholics rarely disagree strongly enough to kill each other; but back in the 16th century thousands and thousands of men, women and children were killed by people who did not agree with their religion.

In the modern world, religious differences can still lead to cruelty and violence. This fact helps us understand the actions of people living 400 years ago.

Life in the past was different

So what do we make of Guy Fawkes' behaviour? It's easy to label him a terrorist because of what he tried to do. But as he himself said in the trial, it is not just wicked people who use violence; good people sometimes have to use violence in their fight against evil.

What is good and what is evil is often a matter of personal opinion. Catholics said Protestant Kings were evil because they led their people to hell. This made it alright to kill them. And Protestants said the same thing about Catholic leaders. Both sides thought they were right.

Today, most of us think both sides were wrong to encourage violence. But we need to guard against believing people who lived 400 years ago thought the same as us. If we want to judge them, we must first understand the very, very different times in which they lived. That's what makes the study of history so fascinating.

Glossary

Accused, the:
Person on trial in a law court

Confess:
Admit to doing wrong

Congregation:
People attending a religious service

Crypt:
Lowest part of a church or cathedral, usually below ground level

Defendant:
Person in court accused of a crime

Dock:
Place in a courtroom where the accused person stands or sits

Earl:
Nobleman

Hue:
Colour

Jury:
Group who decide whether an accused person is guilty or innocent

Plead:
Argue for a particular point of view

Prosecute:
Job of the prosecutor

Prosecutor:
Lawyer whose job is to prove to the jury that an accused person is guilty

Protestant:
Christian who does not accept the leadership of the Pope

Rack:
Instrument of torture that works by stretching the victim

Roman Catholic:
Christian who accepts the Pope as their leader

Verdict:
Decision in a law court – innocent or guilty

Witness box:
Place in a law court where witnesses give their evidence

If you enjoyed reading *Guy Fawkes*, look out for other titles in the series.

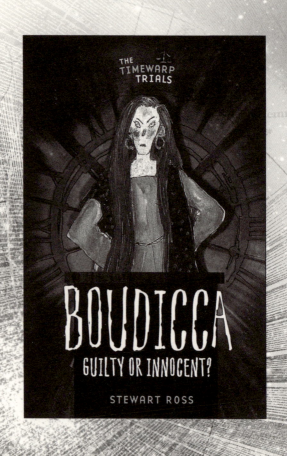

THE TIMEWARP TRIALS

BOUDICCA
GUILTY OR INNOCENT?

STEWART ROSS

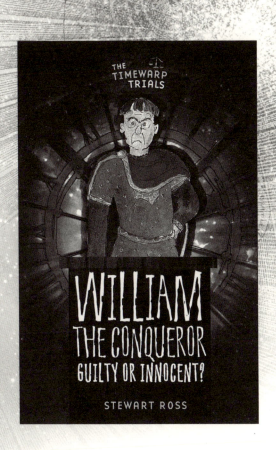

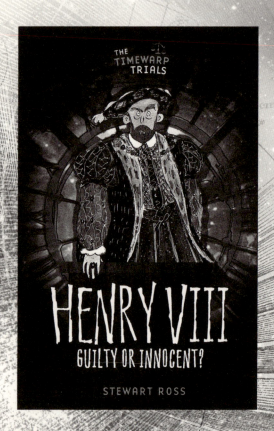

THE
TIMEWARP
TRIALS

HENRY VIII

GUILTY OR INNOCENT?

STEWART ROSS